WHATEVER LIFE

SHOWCASING EXCITING NEW POETS
EDITED BY MICHELLE AFFORD

First published in Great Britain in 2006 by
Spotlight Poets
Remus House
Coltsfoot Drive
Peterborough
PE2 9JX
Telephone: 01733 898101
Fax: 01733 313524
Website: www.forwardpress.co.uk
Email: spotlightpoets@forwardpress.co.uk

SB ISBN 1-84077-157-7

Foreword

Spotlight Poets was established in 1997 as an imprint of Forward Press Ltd in a bid to launch the best of our poets into the public sphere. Since then we have worked hard to present our authors' work in a way that not only complements their style but reflects the class of poet they undoubtedly are.

All the authors in our Spotlight Poets series are hand-selected on the basis of creativity, style and flair, not to mention form and appeal. As a nation of poetry lovers, many of us are still reluctant to venture into the realms of 'new' and 'unknown'. For those of us that would like to take an interest in the poetic art form or for those of us already holding it in high esteem it can be nigh on impossible to find quality new authors and material. Well, we present this to you... Spotlight Poets has opened up a doorway to something quite special.

Within, readers can not only revel in the best of our authors but also take a look at the lives of our poets and what inspires them. Each author has the chance to provide a biography and photograph to allow the reader to take a peek at their contemporaries. As contemporaries ourselves, we love the chance to get involved and take a deeper look at a collection of work. We hope you do too.

Michelle Afford
Editor

Contents

THE POETS & THEIR
FEATURED COLLECTIONS

LAURA CREAN

I am 32 years old, happily married with three beautiful daughters and love writing poetry.

I have always had an inquiring mind; as a child I would ask my mother deep, probing questions like 'If God created the universe, where did God come from?' Writing poetry became my way of making sense of the world, my feelings and my dreams.

Different things interest me and influence my poetry; however, the general theme is fairly philosophical and spiritual. I love reading science fiction, fantasy novels and books about ancient myths and legends, mysterious and paranormal phenomena, archaeology and, my latest passion, psychology. I am currently studying towards a psychology degree with the Open University and find it a very stimulating subject; it makes you look at the world and people in a different way and I hope this will eventually be reflected in my poetry.

I write only for pleasure and when the whim takes me, often I will write after meditating or praying and these are usually the times when a theme for a poem will almost write itself. Watching my children playing, news reports on the television or an interesting subject in a book will also often start my creative writing juices flowing. I write from the heart and my heart tells me if it looks and sounds right. If it flows when I read it back to myself and the words hit a nerve when other people read them, then I'm happy. The fact is I love writing poems and I hope people will love reading them too.

The Tower

Why is it, that since Man began to build,
the bricks and mortar have become a status symbol?
As if continuing to grow, they are so willed,
and beneath its spire all are humble.
It is a symbol of great power
to be a higher being above all others.
To climb the heights of his great tower
is to reach Heaven before his brothers.
Some men get lost when on this great journey,
locked in that ivory tower of seclusion.
They continue in their search, all the while learning
their 'towering intellect' is just an illusion.
As Man observes the view from his skyscraper
his perspective is altered with his height.
These man-made mountains cast such shadows they hamper
the truth of what exists below, for it is out of sight.
And this is why all men of power in church or castle
from spire or turret do survey
the happenings below them that are distorted,
all are carried with the screen of clouds away.
Why is it that in dreams we continue climbing
the never-ending spiral stair?
Never really truly finding
what it is we are looking for up there.
The higher up we carry on our tiring climb
the brighter shines that cleansing light.
And running out of precious time
it is too late to descend back to unwanted night.
And when awaking exhausted from the climbing dream,
the taste of 'more' lingers in the air.
We have touched the gate to Heaven, it may seem,
and all that's left is an ache of wanting to resume our journey there.
Sometimes in our climbing dream
we may lose our balance and start to fall,
only finding when we continue dreaming
we have begun again the climb up that steep wall.
Where does the climbing search for power end?
And is it to be reached through building towers?
Or is it only in the dreams of men,
and the search for Heaven between lovers?

Children Of The Dawn

Father
Time
in Heaven,
wherever that may be
in whatever form or reality,
grant us a diversion from your continuity,
give us all a little peace to savour your piety
and the sight of wisdom to travel your road with dignity.

Mother Earth so patient and tolerant of our sins,
take away the chains of greed and give your children wings
to fly from our short-sightedness and plant the seeds of hope,
may they blossom with love and charity and help lost souls to cope.

Children of the dawn greet the day anew,
absorb the bright sun's energies and savour every view.
Lend a helping hand to keep the stars from falling,
to be the hands of destiny is your only calling.

Yours is the road less travelled,
it is the road of time,
help us now to plan our route
that leads to the
divine.

The Road Less Travelled

If ever you are in some doubt
about your life's direction,
take a large step back
and make a new connection

to all that makes you who you are
and to all those lives you have touched,
it seems you have come so very far
and achieved so much.

If you observed your own life's journey
from a different point of view,
I am sure you would see the difference
you have made to other lives by just simply being you.

Sometimes the road's a long one
with many obstacles along the way,
you have met a fair few crossroads
and had many tolls to pay.

I know the way's not always clear
and you often may get lost,
but just think of those you hold most dear
and not of how much it has cost.

Then start to plan a new journey
and this time take the scenic route,
don't be in such a hurry,
don't follow the traffic just to suit

another who tries to point the way,
it might not be right for you,
taking the road less travelled
may have a nicer view.

Opening The Star-Gate

(After reading 'Signs in the Sky' by Adrian Gilbert)

As above, so below,
The signs are there for all to know,
Unlock the gate with the key of time,
Over Saturn's threshold lies your way and mine.

Orion's clue to the soul's heavenly journey
Is encoded in myths of Man's ancient memory.
And so from Khufu to Peter's reign,
The new custodian of the secret of the same . . .

Jesus knew the message He should teach,
A new age, another chance for Heaven the soul to reach.
But the son of Man is not all he seems,
He is the first and last, the alpha and omega,
So what for mankind could this possibly mean?

At the beginning of the age of the dawn of Adam
From the east the lion reared his royal head.
At the end of the age, the guardian of time
Now comes forth in the lion's stead.

To complete the cycle of Orion's reign,
We must heed the signs in that heavenly chain
And watch for the opening of that symbolic gate
And the Earth-shattering changes it may create.

Now is the ending but also the start
Of a new chain of time and a new change of heart,
We must now unlock that magical door,
Hope is the key but only time can be sure

That we may learn from all our mistakes,
Time is the journey the soul must take.

Dreams Of Flight

I have had the most satisfying dream
since childhood beyond my memory,
the truth behind it and what it really means
is quite a mystery to me.
I have not had the dream of late
since the responsibility of adulthood arrived,
perhaps the innocence and childlike state
is what keeps such dreams alive.
Dreams of flight,
a childish fancy perhaps,
always in a star-filled sky at night,
a time when I can lapse
into a blissful state
of warmth, comfort and security,
a time any babe newly born
from the womb can so relate.
It signifies such innocence, such purity,
perhaps I am reliving a time before my birth,
a time when the love of my mother
was all life's worth.
Or perhaps it was a premonition
of what is waiting beyond the grave,
the mere tinge of a sensation
a soul released from its body can brave.
Or were they just simple
dreams of innocence
in a world where childish whims
die all too soon?
In dreams of flight we can all sense
the freedom and independence
that we brought with us
from the womb.

The Circle Of Truth

I sit within the circle,
the circle of truth.
Amid a swarm of faces
who never give out proof.
I try to look around me
but cannot quite focus on
what is behind the circle's edge,
the truth that lies beyond.

And now begins the lesson,
the reason children sit
within the circle's world of dreams
where they so neatly fit.
The subject of the lesson
is to control what is within.
To capture our true innocence
and disregard all sin.

Each child stands in the middle,
their essence to be found.
The mind and soul a riddle,
around each life is wound.
Now I stand in the circle,
all eyes are turned to me.
I must release the power
and set my spirit free.

I know I will awake soon,
the circle will be gone
and all the children with it,
but we will always be as one.

Realm Of Shadows

I closed my eyes and found a place
where I could lose myself in sleep,
no longer doomed to watch the face,
the dreaded hands of destiny to keep
its slow and steady, infinite pace.

In the realm of shadows
time has not the same intentions,
you may sit undisturbed in quiet meadows
or just be a part of the dream's inventions,
observing, partaking or even moulding
its timelessness to your own ends.

Shadows by their nature follow the real,
holding, copying, mirroring their partner's actions;
often though, the truth it bends,
its distorted path of time can be a distraction,
like the shadow that is extended with the path of the moon!

So it may seem that time has indeed won,
but the realm will not be conquered so soon,
I must take care not to get completely lost,
this place of dreams is a place to observe
and react accordingly, being careful that the boundaries crossed
are straight and true and do not swerve
from the path of this reality,
to intrude on the realm of confusion.

It is easy to lose your way,
in a realm filled with shadows and illusions,
but I know that I can be sure by the light of day
this journey will draw its own conclusions.

The Waters Of Life

My life is moving like a flowing river,
constantly cutting through a path,
it demonstrates a myriad emotions,
it knows that nothing ever lasts.

A quiet stream
may trickle slow and easy,
its calm and gentle whisper
penetrates my dreams.

And yet nothing quite so simple
seems to please me
and nothing quite so complex
seems to tease.

As that sleepy river starts to awaken
and rocks and rapids introduce a change of pace,
I feel my senses sharpen, am I mistaken?
Is my life a river or a race?

And as the rush of water nears its final goal,
the energy of my life force takes a turn,
then suddenly the sum of all my parts are whole,
I feel there is little left I need to learn.

Finally the river finds the ocean,
its vast expanse sets my spirit free
and now I know my mind is open
as the waters of my life mingle with the sea.

So now my soul is moving with the tides of my emotions,
I'm free to ebb and flow in gentle waves
and I know now that my devotion
to my children and my life behaves

just like the ever-changing, ever-flowing
gentle river travelling towards the sea,
and the waters of my life are ever changing,
to suit whatever form it may decide to be.

The Sands Of Time

I sit on the beach and meditate,
the sand between my toes.
I scoop some up and contemplate
the direction my life flows.

Why do my emotions
ebb and flow just like the tides?
And what of my devotion
to mine and my family's lives?

I let the dry sand trickle
through my fingers oh, so slowly,
like when the gentle spring shower tickles
the delicate flowers, I feel almost holy!

I feel a deep appreciation
of my life and its true meaning
and hope my children find their own centre
and the art of simply 'feeling'.

To feel the earth beneath their feet
and the air filling up their lungs,
to taste the salty sea-blown breeze
on their childish tongues.

A Universal Mystery

What is it that my heart is searching for?

It is something I cannot see nor hear and yet it is something more,
a distant shape and a gentle echo that I hold most dear.
Reflections in a moonlit pond, in mists and dew-kissed meadows.
Nature's silent song and the spirit's secret shadows.

What is it that is just beyond my grasp?

It is something I cannot taste nor smell
and yet it is a familiar flavour that is on the tip of my tongue
and fading from my memory fast.
The fragrance of a perfume that I know but cannot name,
the smell of distant memories linger in a room but no one is to blame.

What is it that my soul is yearning for?

It is just around the corner, out of sight but behind an open door.
It is the memories of things to come and the future of things that once were.
The secret name of everything that lives within our sight,
the power of the word, Man has abused this sacred right.
But however hard he whispers his abuse,
you can be sure that God has heard and that Man has tightened his own noose.

What is it that is just beyond my reach?

It is the unimagined,
it is the hopes and fantasies that my dreams are there to try and teach.
It is the hidden wisdom that we ourselves resist,
we lock it in our memories but still it does persist.

The silent, secret universe of the one true Lord, our God
that calls us in our very soul to reach out and break the curse
that Adam did release on us the day he let in sin.
I must reach out to truth and trust that in Jesus now I can enter in.

So that is what my heart was searching for,
that universal mystery behind an open door.
The love of Jesus Christ, my Saviour, has been waiting to come in
to take my hand and lead me through, away from Adam's sin.

GEMMA STEELE

Poetry . . . Poetry means a lot of different things to all of us. I write poetry as an 'emotional release'. Poetry allows me to control my feelings, whether they are bad or good, and allows me to express the emotion that I am feeling. The majority of the poetry that I write tends to be quite dark and depressing, however, I do write different styles of poetry such as love poetry and life poetry.

They say that your childhood has a lot of effect on you in later life and this shows in my work. However, I find that the poetry helps me in dealing with these issues and those that later arise.

I am currently studying in Birmingham for a degree in early years of education studies, and I am hoping to go on and work with children in the future. I'm pretty much a happy-go-lucky kind of girl but I always seem to hit a bit of trouble and this is where poetry comes in and saves my sanity! I am a published poet and my work has been published in several different anthologies. I hope that you enjoy my poetry in this anthology. Some of this work is published and some is unpublished.

I don't have that many ambitions in life, but I would like my work to become more recognised and for people to understand poetry and its meaning as it has been a huge help to me. Another ambition of mine is just to be happy! I am currently very happy, and I hope it stays this way for a very long time!

As Simple As That

Sat here, itching, longing for control
My body's aching, right through to the soul
Just one. That's all I need
Just one. To make me bleed

Blood oozing out the slit
When all I can do is stare and sit
Frozen still. To the spot
Feeling shaky, cold yet hot

Scraping, dragging, pushing deep
Redness forms, watch it seep
Watching it, drip and roll
And all the time, I know I'm in control

All the time, I control what goes on
No one can stop me, not even Mom
This is mine, and no one can change that
But why do I need to cut my skin with tat?

Push it in deep and drag it along
Takes my mind to where I belong
Safe and happy, away from it all
Yet why do I still seem to fall?

I come back down with a great big thud
If everyone knew, my name would be mud
You know I can't help it, and that bit is true
I don't want to feel like this, I don't want to feel blue

I want to feel better, I want to feel happy
But I can't, it's as simple as that

Alone

All alone, I sit and cry
Waiting till the time I die
No one here to hold me tight
In this world, I have to fight

It's just so tough to live like this
All the people who have gone, I miss
What did I do to make them go?
They have hurt me, they'll never know

People around, yet I feel so alone
All I can do is cry and moan
Life doesn't seem worth living at all
It's pulling me deeper . . . I'm gonna fall

Fall into a deep dark pit
My heart broken, bit by bit
Let me go, let me die
I want to go up to the sky

The Sting

Feeling the pain, stinging so deep
Pushing the razor blade, as I weep

I lie stranded on the floor
Feet pushed, against the door

Watching the mark, appear so fast
My mind racing back to the past

Blood dripping down my arm
Now I start to see my harm

Left with a mark so deep and red
Then I slip silently back into bed

Feeling the sting, the pain so immense
Making my body feel so tense

Living by the knife, only way I know
I'm gonna move on, and try let go

Pain

Every time I close my eyes
I see you with her
You're happy and you're smiling
Looks like this is your year

You seem to have it all
You left me here with none
Picked me up, put me down
F****d around, then gone

Wasn't I all you could ever want?
I thought I was everything you could ever need
But it's obvious now
You had to fulfil your greed

You took my heart
And made it strong
To break it after
That was wrong

Why make it strong
To break it soon after?
While I'm in pain crying
All I see from you is laughter

How can you be so happy
When I'm so down?
How can you smile
When I can only frown?

How could you do this to me?
You declared to me your love
Obviously what you felt
It was something but not love

Me

Pretty green eyes
A pink freckled face
Dark flowing hair
Curls in their place

A fixated smile
To hide all the pain
A ton of make-up
To keep me sane

Small petite ears
A little button nose
Soft luscious lips
The colour of rose

This is me
This is real
But how I look
Is not how I feel

No Going Back

Once something is done, it can't be changed
You made the choice, it can't be rearranged

Things are done for a reason, and that must stand
Even if things aren't super, or even grand

That choice was made, and that must stay true
No one can change it now, not even you

There's no going back, never will be
It will be OK in the end, you will see

But what you have to do now is live your life to the max
Never look back, always forward, don't hide your tracks

For life goes forward, not backwards to the past
Live life to the full, for it goes too fast

The End

I'm so afraid
To let you know
About my past
I'll never show

It hurts too much
You'll never see
How much damage
It's done to me

How can I not
Look into your eyes
When all I can see
Is not truth, but lies?

I've come to a conclusion
And this has to be said
For me not to hurt anymore
I'd have to be dead!

Confusion

I can't quite explain
The way you make me feel
It's just so amazing
The feeling is unreal

You make me feel I'm glowing
I feel so warm inside
You make me feel so special
Yet these feelings I have to hide

For if I could, I'd be with you
And happy I would be
Life would be so splendid
I would feel contented, you and me

But I just don't know what's right for you
Or even what you want
All I know is that you make feel this way
And the feeling is one I want

New Year's Resolution 2003-2004

A new year
A new start
Don't dwell
Or break a heart

Live life to the full
Be a good friend
Work hard in life
You never know when it will end

Don't feel guilt
It's not your fault
Don't feel hurt
Like wounds and salt

Be honest and truthful
And be as one
Do as you please
Life's not a con

Life is precious
Special and true
Life's for living
And not feeling blue

Remember in the end
A broken heart can *always* mend

Burning Desire

A feeling so warm
Of burning inside
To hide the desire
Oh how I've tried

An aching inside
Yet it feels so good
Who'd have thought
Pain ever could?

This burning desire
For want and for need
This burning desire
Will I ever succeed?

The loving I crave
And want so much
Your lips on mine
Your caressing touch

This burning desire
Is tearing me apart
This burning desire
My broken heart

Feelings
(Dedicated to Jed)

Only yesterday we were together
But it feels so long ago
I can still feel your arms around me
Still hear your voice so low

See your happy smiling face
In this mind of mine
I wanna be there always
Never draw the line

I feel so much for you
I just hope that you know
Forever and for always
Never let me go

Happy and contented
Is what you make me feel
I can't believe I feel this way
The whole thing is just surreal

Baby, I care for you so much
I don't think you have a clue!
I thought that I should tell you
I'm falling in love with you!

Forever
(Dedicated to Jed)

I can't think of a better place
That I would like to be
I can't think of a better person
That I would like to see

Happiness is everlasting
Never to an end
Contentment also covered
To my every need, you tend

In your arms, safe and warm
A feeling of pure bliss
A feeling so good never goes away
When I'm gone, this is what I miss

This is how I want to stay
Forever and for always
Want to stay happy with you
Till the end of my days

My Wish

Admiration, hope and care
Living a life, I want to share
I can see it now, me and you
Living a life that feels so true

Never a moment, without sweetness and light
Tucked up together silently, night by night
I want to be with you, more than life itself
Feelings so strong, never felt it myself

I want all this with you, and plenty more
I wanna be with you, for eternity I'm sure
I'm not feeling love, but that will come
Time will tell, move on, have some fun

So, darling, let's do this together
Be happy, free, joyous together
Make my night and be with me
Love me eternally and make my soul free

KEVIN COOK

Kevin Cook was born in 1963 and grew up in Bedfordshire. After leaving school, he became a carpenter and still carries on with this trade today.

His pastimes are drawing, writing, shooting and skiing.

Today he still lives in Bedfordshire and has children of his own. At present he is working on short stories as well as his poetry.

In The Beginning

In the end,
The beginning is so strong,
It makes you wonder,
What went wrong.
Depressed and alone,
Needing so much,
It is not hard to understand,
The need to be touched.

In the end,
Thoughts of passion and lust.
In the days,
Now lost and gone,
Now with another,
You're still there.
Your presence sometimes,
Makes it hard to bear.

In the end,
Which is so near,
Anything could happen,
So I will leave this here.
The world is full of people,
Odd, strange and queer.
It can only get better,
The future is here.

Time Called

Tortured mind,
Body in pain.
Will my life ever be the same . . . ?
Is it fate,
Or is it me?
I have a feeling
It is just meant to be.
Try a little harder?
I do not think so!
I have done my best,
Now it is time to go.

Set Her Free (And Me)

I loved her,
I freed her,
I finally let her go.
She rings,
She calls,
But I'll not answer her.
She had me,
She lost me,
Now I have let her go.
No more loving,
From the one she truly knows.
Her way or my way,
Now it is time to part.
Time maybe,
For new partners,
To mend our damaged hearts.
My love's not instant,
It has a magic of its own.
Its spells take time,
To wipe away the hurt.
But, she's not waiting,
She's stamping on my heart.
And now,
After all these years,
It's time for us to part.

Going East And West

Do not walk away,
Do not turn your back.
I think I deserve,
More than that.
The years have tolled their toll,
It is easy to see,
Life's a little harder than watching TV.
So stop your madness,
Your wanting ways.
Please, take my hand,
Walk this way.

Open Soul

Here I stand,
Naked and bare.
Come on, people,
Have a good stare.
Cover yourselves up,
In what's not you.
I feel like an animal
Locked in a zoo.
The whole world is mine,
But I am still trapped.
So come on, people,
Think on that.
You do not understand
All, I feel.
You just look at me,
With eyes that could kill.
Now leave me alone,
I'm not at my best.
I am tired,
I am lonely,
Now leave me to rest.

Missin'

The love of my life,
The bringer of pain.
My life's in a mess,
Yes, we have split once again.
No more trust,
But a heart full of pain.
I wait in my madness,
In sorrow I am chained.

Shining Knight

When I look
Into your eyes,
I wish,
I hope,
But not to die,
But to lie in your arms
For evermore,
For all of time,
Please . . .
Maybe more.
My heart,
My body,
Soul and mind
Are in your hands,
So hold them tight
And hold them safe,
For you're the one,
To make my heart race.
Without your love,
Your touch,
Your breath,
My life would be a mess.
So don't let go,
Just hold me tight,
And I will be
Your shining knight.

Listen To Me (Please)

I told you so,
That I was low.
I told you so,
That you were wrong.
I told you so,
It would be hard.
I told you so,
We have far to go.
I told you so,
That you were not right.
People give in,
I am here to fight.
I told you so, I love you.
I told you so,
That this would pass.
I told you so,
I would say goodbye.

Menorca Thoughts

A warm breeze is felt,
Across the water's edge.
Romance is felt,
Inside my head.
Thoughts of you
On sunny days,
Lift my heart,
And make me smile,
To remember the good times,
We had for a while.
Sand between toes,
A dance by the moon,
It should have lasted longer,
Not ended so soon.
Now for a while,
It is back to life and dreams.
But my thoughts of your body,
Are sharp and keen.

Sandcastles And Tide

Sandcastle against the tide,
That's what me and you are.
I build walls with good faith,
Then in comes your tide
To destroy
The progress we have made.
To wash away our sandcastle walls,
Leaving holes that will take time to fill.
But now,
Like tsunami,
You have come in this time
For the kill,
Flattening all,
And all for a thrill.
Now I have to swim away from you,
To find a place of rest,
A place to build my sandcastle walls.
A place away
From the turmoil you cause.

A Father's Thoughts

Now grown up,
A woman to be.
It is only now
I begin to see.
You are my daughter,
My pride, my heart, my soul,
The love of my life, I did, I believe,
Tell you so.
Now it is time to let you go,
To live your life as you see fit.
So please do not be rash,
In the things you do,
And always remember, Daughter,
Your father loves you. *xx*

Untitled

The feeling of weight upon me,
Pushed deep in my bed.
Sheets creased and rumpled,
Thoughts of angels
In my head.
I feel my body tremble,
I feel myself alive.
These feelings long lost,
Awakened now,
Bring a tear to my eyes,
You make me ache
When you are near.
For a period of time
I had not feared,
Engrossed in another,
Lost, floating and free,
I hope my future stays happy,
I hope my mind stays clear.

Untitled

Three generations,
Side by side.
When you look at the photo,
Do you wonder about time?
A father's love,
Through and through,
Passed on down,
From me to you.
Look to the future,
It is soon to come.
Not long from now,
You will have *your* son.

JEANNINE ANDERSON HALL

My poetry is dedicated to my darling youngest child, Sheralyn Hall (July 20th 1951 - March 21st 1973), several were written after the loss of my beloved husband, George Hall, in 1997.

Born in Lancaster, the only child of Margaret and Percival Anderson, I came to Blackpool at an early age, where I still reside. I have a son and two other daughters. Although I live alone my faith sustains me, and has enabled me to write my poetry collection which I have entitled 'The Flowers Of Heaven'.

Flowers Of Heaven

You were so sweetly gentle when you left,
Adorned in nature's loveliest.
And all the sunshine of my days was in your smile,
Its warmth enfolded me awhile.

Then as you passed,
The flowers of Heaven perfumed the air,
And mirrored in your lovely eyes,
Unspoken was the promise,
Of awaiting me in paradise.

Golden Girl

My bonnie girl, my golden girl
Not one is like to thee,
And in answering smile lay your reply
Many are fashioned so!

But if in game you hid yourself among them, every one,
In a moment I would find you,
For who knows not their own?
Oh! Bonnie girl, my golden girl, did Heaven think as I?
You were lent so short a time,
Yet I'll not question why.
For through such a gift reclaimed,
Another one is given,
When I this earthly sphere must leave,
No dread shall overpower,
No void but light,
To banish any fear.
And there in Heaven, 'midst angel throngs
In a moment, you, I'll find - and run to,
Clasp you in my heart and in my aching arms,
For in the truth of that sweet moment
You will surely understand,
That as before and evermore,
Are you to me - my bonnie girl, my golden girl,
Not one is like to thee.

Confidence

What shall I fear now you are gone?
Shall it be some dread of yesteryear
Will creep up unawares,
Or for tomorrow's need which may
Bring fresh grief or care?
No! I shall take today, each minute sanctify,
For what ought I fear now,
Fear fled to naught, but you
To paradise.

Waiting

Though I have gone before you
I have not travelled far,
Just reached Heaven before you
So for me you must be glad.
And though 'twas hard to leave you
My heart was filled with joy,
For I have entered into paradise
And everlasting life.

Together

For you are part of me and I of you,
And till with you can share eternity,
With faith can share your Heaven,
And you with certainty, my Earth.

Love's Whisper

If some should wonder why,
I accept not you are gone,
The answer lies deep in my heart
And mind,
Your voiceless words tell me
There is no death,
You still live on!

Trust

I shall not despair without you
To have and to hold,
I shall not weep too much
For you've been spared the growing old!
And what was once the feared
Unknown has ceased to be,
For all the lovely things you were
Proves immortality!

Forever Together

We shall never be apart, my love,
You have not lost my heart,
For I am always with you,
Though all around seems dark.
Speak to me in silent words,
For I can hear your thoughts,
Reach out to me and know, my love -
You'll never be alone.

Blessed Child

It would seem that when a child is taken
All the world would weep its deepest tears,
Yet when with gentle care and tenderness
Were you, enfolded in our hearts, laid to your rest,
There was no rain to prove it so,
The sun had shed its radiance over all.
And there had been no need for rain!
For as we smiled when first you came,
So did Heaven, on your return.

Love's Promise

Though grief embrace, it should be doubly mine
That all the glory I now see,
One glimpse I cannot give to thee.

And for my loss thou would'st not pine
Nor shed vain tears in after years,
But spend thine own allotted time
To merit such a wondrous sphere.

Then we shall be together in these
Bright celestial climes,
And face to face see Heaven
In each other's eyes.

Until

Time holds no meaning for me now
Except to mark the hours as it has always done.
So precious it had been when spent
With you, but you are gone,
Out from the marking of a day into
The timeless realms of beauty,
Perchance, from whence you came.
To think on this, then precious life remains
To spend in gaining merit for eternal things.
For could the answer to the life of
Someone's unfair role, may be in truth,
That each has their own part to play
And prove oneself, as you have done,
Then be reclaimed for infinite glory,
Endless day, eternal love.

Innocents

In the far reaches of the most learned mind
No answer could one find to senseless massacre.
Down through the ages echoes still
The lament of Rachael, weeping
For her children, comfortless!
But God is never mocked!
These deeds are written in eternity,
Each word is bold and clear
And naught shall hide one letter of them,
Like the doers blot the Earth.
Paradise throws wide its gates to slaughtered innocents,
They are numbered among its saints
And have the playground of the universe
Awaiting those who mourn them
With garlands made of each tear shed,
And a crown of glory for their grief.

Light In Darkness

How beautiful the starlit sky
As if with brightest lamps,
The angels keep their loving watch
O'er mortals here on Earth.

And could it be, that if a star
Should fall and seeming die,
A new soul rises in rebirth,
And all the stars will ever shine
In Heaven's eternal radiance?

The Blessing

Day's loveliest gown,
The cloak of velvet night, adorned
With stars of brilliant profusion,
Like new souls from Earth
Shine forth last benedictions,
And, come the dawn, pass on -
Into the eternal light of Heaven.

Hope

Though now my days seem endless night,
For you an everlasting dawn has broken,
And to one hope I cling through all my sorrow -
Though I know not the time
When we shall meet again,
For you - it will seem tomorrow!

Lost Child

Now, after deep despair like blackest night
Through blinding mist of tears shine
Rays of hope-filled light.
To see the night fade into bright new dawn,
And faith, within the heart reborn -
Which tells the certainty of Heaven.

'Tis not cruel fate removes a child from Earth,
'Tis God! His favoured one reclaims,
Thus shows the path He knows we'll surely take,
The end of which our darling waits!

Faith

Beloved, I remember thee,
Pray, love, remember me,
That the tears I have shed,
And the heart that has bled,
Shall not have been in vain.

Though you need them not
May the weight of the cross, which
I willingly bear with its pain,
Keep me on the path in the
Footsteps you trod and, like you,
I will Heaven gain.

Until

Though we must walk apart awhile,
In this world made darker with your loss,
I should not weep,
For if but faith can keep,
Know you with angels walk
Till I with you, my love -
In paradise above.

Angels

Angels drift around us,
As like a gentle breeze,
Sweet messengers and guardians
From glorious realms unseen.

We may not see or hear them
Yet they enfold us in their love,
And whisper words which tell us,
Where we should strive to go.

Forever

They are not just a memory
Our loved ones gone before,
They are just beyond our sight
And we shall meet once more.

And all the tears of yesterday
All grief and pain will be no more,
For we shall be together,
Never to part again.

DONALD DAVIDSON

I was born in Bermondsey, South London, the youngest of a family of eleven, although I only knew three brothers and four sisters. My hardworking mother lost some of her offspring through several difficult mishaps. I was spoiled by one sister, and treated like a slave by brothers who did not want another kid in the house. I was told that on the day I was born, I was placed in a drawer on top of the neatly starched sheets ready for the pawn shop on Monday. One of my brothers looked at me in disappointment and said, 'What's that?' then slammed the drawer shut. My life, I am afraid!

I was a loner with only one friend who sadly died in 2002 and I miss him more than I do any of my siblings. Only one sister is alive, she is eighty-four, a war bride living in Canada. I am married with one daughter, Donna, who has given me the pleasure of two grandchildren, Samantha and Stephen, whom I spoil incessantly, as is my right.

I served in the RAF but my time there was a disaster just waiting to happen, definitely not for a scrawny kid from the slums of Bermondsey, and best forgotten. I spent my working life in the printing industry, until an accident at work ended my days of employment. Then I dabbled in rhymes, using any subject as my theme.

I made friends with B, a lovely lady who is happily married and possibly the most unlikely person I should have ever met, but meet we did and we became good friends. I enjoy my friendship with her because we hide nothing from each other. My main theme now is my love for her as my most treasured gift; a friend who came into my life, showing me that nothing is impossible. Her influence has given me a plausible reason to write and, possibly, I take full advantage of her friendship. I can tell her of my life as a scruffy cockney kid from a very large family, and she has given me a perspective of hers as an only child born to a naval family, enjoying the sunshine of Malta. 'A modern day beauty and the beast' possibly.

I enjoy the challenges of writing in rhyme and find it very easy but the strange thing is, it is only since B and I became friends.

Friends

If I was asked at some other time
To explain what I mean by my friend
I would have to think for quite a while
Before giving the reply that I intend
The word 'friend' to my way of thinking
Cannot easily be explained as it might
So if I did have to reply to that question
I would need to make sure I was right
In my mind there is no end to friendship
No barrier will be too vast
I could not call you my friend for one moment
If I expected that moment to pass
I have a place deep down inside me
A special place which I intend
To keep available until that time
I would need it for a friend
A friend will give and ask nothing in return
Intend no sorrow or pain
Yet friendship received is a profit
That exceeds any monetary gain
So I will look forward to the time that I am asked
To explain what I mean by my friend
For I certainly know what my answer will be
In just two simple words . . .
No end!

Of Love

I held her hand, a loving hand
Tender, though worn through the years
I could feel on her finger a small gold band
And my eyes were filled with tears.
I glanced at her hair, a silvery crown
And her face looked so tired and old.
I held my breath, for the hand that I held
Had suddenly turned very cold.
With tears in my eyes, I thought back through the years
Of a time that could not possibly last
When she had nursed all my ailments and I held back my tears
But the feeling of love was so vast.
She had given the best years of her life
With joy in her heart for me
Then without a murmur, a sound or a cry
My mum just ceased to be.
I could see that peace had come at last
Her lifetime of stress at an end
And God had called my mum to His side
Because He needed a friend.
It is said that there is an afterlife
And the life that we bear
Is the life that this one should have been
So I kissed her brow, and stroked her hair
My mum will be a queen . . .

Age And Distance!

I really do not mind the fact
That I am much older than you
Of course I would prefer it not to be the case
And five years or maybe just two
Were separating my age from yours
For then I would really try
To steal you away to my promised land
But . . . maybe too many years have gone by
I find now that as I grow older
The feelings I have in my heart
Could be possibly seen as a reason
For keeping us both apart
No matter what age or what distance
Is between us now and, maybe, my end
I love you deeply in a special way
Tenderly. A love for a friend
There can then be no such thing as age or time
No distance will be too much
As a friend I can crave for the smile in your eyes
And yearn for your soft tender touch
So please, friend, forgive me for the way that I feel
If you think that this feeling is new
You are, of course, right. It comes from within
But only since the day I met you.

Never Without Me

Can you feel it? That we are friends
Close. As good friends should be,
Do you, as I do, feel that warming bond?
My heart knows it is there but my eyes do not see.
Will we always be close? Now and into beyond?
In this time while I feel you and I are one . . .
Could there ever be a better time not to feel alone?
Bonded together like the Earth and the sun.
Do you feel at times feel I am intense? And yet
I cling tightly onto friendship, while we live as two,
How sad it would have been, had we never met.
Do you at times feel that I am a burden to you?
Yet I know we are close, regardless of all adversity,
I have memories guarded here inside my heart,
I bring them out to comfort me on lonely days,
And give me hope when we are apart.
I feel it deep within my soul, we are special.
You are my dearest friend, I love you
So you will always be
Kept safe where you need never feel alone
And never without me . . .

For B

(With gratitude and love for her friendship)

One day without you in my life
Leaves me feeling alone and in despair.
One day without the sight of your face
Or not seeing the glow in your hair.
One more day without you
And I can't see the smile in your eyes
Or my heart does not seem to beat
Or my breath comes out in sighs.
I do not want one more moment
When I would notice you were not there
If only you missed me as I do you
Then you would know just how much I do care.
If I have to live through one more day with no you in it
Here and now I must say
All my hope and my life will have ended
If you are not there on any one day.

A Thought

One thought fills my mind
The wonder that is you
I need to hold you close and then I will know
That this dream is true
I want to touch you or all I will feel
Is an ache or a loss or a pain
How is it I can hold such dreams
Until you are close again?
There really is no reason
Why I should feel so sad
When most of the thoughts that are in my mind
Are the loveliest I have ever had
But then again, when I am alone
I am filled with a feeling of fear
In case I lose that loving touch
Or I don't feel you near
Pity me as I hold out my love
For you to keep in your heart
For thoughts of you will stay in mine
That way we will never part . . .

Loss Of Love

If when you have read through this ode
My sadness has taken its toll
Remember please that while I have known you
I have loved you, body and soul
During happier times while we have been friends
If you have felt a need for me
Thank you, but while you have been out of my sight
My eyes have had no reasons to see
For if I could not breathe from the air that you breathed
Nor gaze at the blue in your eyes
Nor feel your heart beat as you stood close to me
Then this parting will bring no surprise
But if, at times, you did feel a need for me
And you felt my love in your heart
You will know that I love you more than my life
And you will feel the loss now that we have to part
In the light of the moon, and the warmth of the sun
By night and by day I did care
And the loss I now feel for the smile that I crave
Is far too much for my broken heart to bear
God, in love, brought me to you
But in that moment He tore us apart
Sadly He showed me His darker side
As slowly He has torn out my heart
Love freely given and blessed by Him
But taken without saying why
Seems so cruel and cannot be forgotten
For in life true love should not die
Memories of you will stay with me forever
I know what I have lost now we part
You are my B, that can never now change
For B is the name of my heart.

MARJ BUSBY

I have been writing for what seems forever, the most recent poetry being published with Forward Press. I have been in three other Spotlight books and several New Fiction books. I keep saying this is my last but I can't resist just one more! I have found Forward Press most helpful and encouraging and it is a pleasure to be associated with them.

I have been published in a lot of anthologies in America and England. Also magazines in England and Australia where I now reside, but I still remain a British citizen. I have never become a naturalised Australian.

I mainly write for my family which is now quite large. By giving them the books I am in, I feel that they will have something to remember me by in future when I am no longer with them all. Plus, I have a lot of American and English friends who always clamour for a copy of my latest ones. I cannot always oblige but they take turns. I suppose one day I'll dry up but will keep going as long as I am able.

A Day With Nature

Clouds, fluffy-white, riding the sky.
A beautiful canopy for the landscape below.
Green the grass, blue the lake,
On which small boats are bobbing like corks.
Wanderers on the grass, enjoying nature's pleasures.

Couples, arms entwined, walk the paths,
Around the lake on which white swans
Arch their necks regally, sailing with elegance.
Magnificent a sight, as people watch it all,
Knowing that their life is made up of such treasures.

Just an ordinary day in summer,
No thoughts of war at that moment.
Thinking of nothing else but the beauty,
As they enjoy their day out with nature.
Getting a generous fill of all its measures.

Any Dream Can Come True

Any dream can come true,
if you long for it to happen.
Even a broken dream also,
can make you feel less blue.

That one you love too much
who doesn't seem to love you,
can change his wandering heart,
then you can tremble at his touch.

It's a game lovers play,
one day you seem to be a fool.
Another, you open wide your eyes,
and suddenly it's your big day.

So close together, you'll no longer feel blue,
as together you finally join as one.
Dressed in white, carrying a bouquet,
you will find your dream's come true.

A Rose So Red

Roses that give so much delightful pleasure,
Fill our hearts with so much love.
I have received many over countless years,
The sweetest being a beautiful red treasure.

The perfume that emanated from it, giving out power,
To fill my heart with love like no other.
For it came from my one and only true lover.
The one that made my whole body flower.

It was delivered in a box, shaped as a heart,
Looking at it long, it finally had to fade.
Now it is locked in my treasure chest,
Full of mementoes from which I can never part.

Broken Dreams

Like an arrow piercing a heart,
for lovers living far apart.
Torment, longing for a loving arm,
never knowing, there might be harm.

Thoughts, making happiness fitful and sparse.
Ideals lost, amidst strife, a farce.
Surely dreams sometimes do come true?
Mending the cracks, healing, long overdue.

Longings, being fearful, hopeful, hardly ever.
Was love meaning them to sever forever?
Still their hope lingers, heading away screams,
for one day, hopefully, no broken dreams.

Fantasy

Moon casting a white light
Fireflies gleaming in its height.
Fairies dancing with delight
Elves being mischievous and bright.

Come join their merry band
See the fairy queen, wand in hand.
Feel as if the world is at its best
Forget your troubles, live with zest.

For soon morning will arrive
People hoping they can survive.
The horrors of the coming day
Wishing only that night would stay.

Try and live in the fantasy of this night
Believe you see those creatures so bright.
Trusting that sanity will return without cost
Just enjoy what is happy, don't think all is lost.

First Love

When you fall in love,
It may not be forever.
Those sweet kisses that enthral,
Make you think you are clever.

Sometimes first love is just a trial,
Love can fade, fly away like a dove,
Another lover may take your fancy.
Still, enjoy those early kisses of love.

When some other love comes along,
Think back to that first encounter.
For never again will a kiss feel so sweet,
As your first loving romancer.

For All The Lonely

Do not despair that love will come
For often it lurks in funny places.
Smile and think how lucky you are
Able to work, walk, and talk to strange faces.
So get out and about, talk to all you meet.
Soon you will find friends that are keen,
To make your life happy again, as you smile,
Then life will seem brighter than it's ever been.

He Had To Help

Stepping out into the dark night,
My eyes focus upon one bright star.
Blackness of the night suiting my plight,
For I feel forsaken, with my lover gone afar.

The brightness of one heavenly star in time.
Realising our hearts in love, being refined,
Never thinking that there, feeling sublime
Our feelings so attuned as one, entwined.

Now that I'm alone, looking at this bright light,
My lover no longer by my side,
For he has gone afar, leaving me with fright,
Although promising to return as I, my tears, hide.

So, lonely, I gaze at this dark sky.
Imagining that the lonely star in my sight,
Is my lover, helping others not to die,
Easing my heart, knowing as I wait, he was right.

Life

Life is bitter, leaving an acrid taste.
Why are we born to start to die?
For what reason do years of life waste?
Better never to have lived, it all seems a lie.

What use the years, the effort of living?
Birth, crying, laughing, happiness, sadness.
To what purpose is all the loving and giving?
Somehow the whole scheme of life seems madness.

Peeping At Spring

Trees begin to show leaves,
delicate shades of green.
Shrouding the brown trunks,
making one's heart feel light.

Gone the winter cold,
fingers and toes that felt raw.
Chimneys no longer belching smoke,
making sunlight appear more clear.

The park shows flowers bright,
children play, one tries to catch a butterfly.
Toddlers stumbling, stagger upright and walk,
golden marigolds glow, giving a light.

Such weather pleases all
as they go about their ways.
Seemingly to walk taller
as holidays spring to mind.

Spring comes only once a year,
for when it's over, summer's arrived.
Warmth pervades bodies cool,
people stop to linger and chat.

Spring welcomes all lovers,
as they quietly walk in the park.
Welcomed by all this weather,
winter forgotten, love in their hearts.

My Love

How much I did love you, all those years gone by,
Never ever thinking that one day, one of us would die.
Those walks we took together in summertime,
Our words to one another making a special rhyme.
Although I loved you dearly, back in days of long ago,
Never thinking about when age became reality, that feeling's
Still in memory at least, you are still my love supreme,
I did not notice your greying hair or lines so extreme.
And so we were together for many, many years.
Now that you have left me, I do not waste time in tears.
For still I recall your bright red hair, your eyes so blue,
I have always retained in memory, a picture that is just you.

Night-Time Flights

When the moon is aglow,
I fly all the night long.
Visiting places of long ago,
Flying high, I can do no wrong.

I treasure these lovely flights,
When I meet, and sink into a lover's bed.
For we find again our past delights.
Forgetting the memory that they are dead.

As the sun begins to rise
I return to the land of the living.
Feeling not weary, to my surprise.
Just happiness, loving and giving.

I long for arms to again enfold me,
Lips pressed to mine, so sweet.
A body to nestle with and see,
That I am cocooned, as we do meet.

Old Memories

She walked into the greenest field
it produced a feeling of inner peace.
This aged crone did feel a sense
of inward pressure, that did not yield.

Wandering across to a wooden stile
where once she and her lover had stood.
Memories came flooding, she fell to her knees
feeling caresses of long ago, making her smile.

As she unsteadily arose, still in the past
making her journey back across the field.
Her steps began to feel so very light
as, dying, she went to join her lover at last.

Viennese Scenes

Trees of the Vienna woods
Are so varied and colourful a treasure.
Strauss music, 'Tales of the Vienna Woods'
Makes one's heart beat faster with pleasure.

Such differing hues and magnificent stature
One wonders who designed such delights.
Trees red, yellow and green, weeping willows
Bring to hearts, raising them to such heights.

One has to go far to find a better sight
But a journey well worth the final scene.
For in every tree, is the work of God's hand
There to enjoy and never regret what has been seen.

CAROLINE TURNER

This is a first for me and you will have to excuse me if I laugh a little at the very thought of a profile on me.

Who am I? Well I started life in London in the year 1945. I was the last of five daughters and I like to think that it was at this point that my father gave up any hope of a son and settled for me. I grew to be taller and stronger than any of my siblings, and in later years, when both my parents died, I became the parent they turned to in times of difficulty.

I am married to the gentlest man, who is very patient, unlike myself, I tend to want things done as fast as possible. A sort of 'never put off till tomorrow what can be done today' type of person.

I don't know when writing poems started; it's just one of the things I do. Usually I write about people I know or things in life pertaining to me or my family and friends. I don't think of myself as a poet, just as someone trying to make people laugh or get over a sad time.

A few years ago I tentatively put forward a poem with encouragement from my husband, Alan, and was greatly surprised to have it accepted for publication. Since then I have sent in an odd one here and there. Recently, however, I wrote one for my keep-fit instructor who published it in the local monthly magazine. This has led to a very surprised me showing some of my work to friends; something that I have never done before. I have received so much encouragement from these dear people that I thought I owed it to myself and to them to submit my work for Spotlight Poets

A Circle Of Life

Another year over the nursery stage
Gone from our life like the turn of a page
A few weeks of summer
With smiles, love and laughter
Preceding the trauma of school that comes after
That first day with hands clutched. No wish to let go
Then gradually confidence soon it will show
They're running to school now, got no time to wave
No need to say 'careful', no need to 'be brave'
They saunter away with their thoughts on their friends
And what they will play when the lesson time ends
It's time to step back, give advice when it's needed
To see if the lessons you taught them have seeded
Then into a routine; school, sleep, holiday, play
How it goes on and on until finally, one day
The child disappears and the adult arrives
A new game begins as development thrives
It's colleges, courting and then the big day
Marriage with children is well underway
The circle completes as the little ones grow
From baby to toddler their characters flow
Till soon they have reached the big nursery age
A year down the line and they're over that stage
You know what comes next as you've done it before
Though it's hard to step back when your child's not so sure
For now you're the parent who's been once removed
Watching with love and with memories accrued
So that, friend, is life, never ending or done
A continual circle of love, life and fun

Maybe A Blessing In Disguise

When your 'get up and go'
Has got up and gone
And washing and dressing
Is taking too long
Look out of the window
And up at the sky
Then sit quietly and watch
As the white clouds float by
You'll soon see the sun
As it stirs from its bed
And you'll feel its strong warmth
As its rays touch your head
The breeze will feel good
As you open the window
And breathe in the fragrance
Of flowers you've watched grow
As birds, bees and butterflies
Flutter around
You'll see all their colours
Yet not hear a sound
So what if it takes time
For washing and dressing
In our beautiful world
Taking time is a blessing

Love

How much do I love you?
Can I show you the way?
I've loved you for a lifetime
Every minute, every day
From the first time that I met you
You have filled my every thought
I don't think you'll ever realise
How much joy to me you brought
Through the good and through the bad times
You've stood by me, quiet and strong
Your arms there to protect me
When it seemed that things went wrong
Without question - without reason
With love always in your eyes
In your smile and in your actions
In your truth - you told no lies
Every time you have to leave me
How it breaks my heart in two
I'm not whole, I'm all in pieces
When I'm torn apart from you
How much do you think I love you?
Can I ever show the way?
All I know for sure, my darling
It's until my dying day

Alone

As a solitary being, we enter this life
If lucky we're loved from the start
With a mother, a father, maybe sister or brother
The bonds that don't sever apart

Yet even with these, a good life, lots of friends
Happy family, plus a good home
We can all try to hide, in pretence or in pride
But in truth, we are always alone

We can fill up our time with our hobbies and pets
Spend each minute, each day in a crowd
We can hide from the fact that we're lonely inside
Throwing parties or laughing out loud

But beneath the façade, and although it is hard
Who'll admit even when we're full-grown?
When it comes down to life, when we enter or leave
Well! We just have to do it alone

Hurt

Why does it hurt when a friend tells a lie
And why does it feel like you just want to cry?
Why does it hurt when your love says goodbye
And why does it feel that you just want to die?
Why does it hurt when you fall to the floor
And why are you left so embarrassed and sore?
Why do folk that we love have to leave
And why do we smile when we just want to grieve?
Why do we feel that we just must not show
The feelings we have when our life's at a low?
Why can't we talk when we feel our heart's breaking
And where is the hug when our body is shaking?
Hurt is a feeling we need to erase
Else it sours up our lives for the rest of our days

High Society

I do not envy folk like you
You can't help who you are
In your own eyes
You've got it made
You're certain you'll go far

That's not to say that I won't too
But by another track
Don't cast me off without a glance
And never once look back

For money maketh no man
And we've all been put on Earth
To live our lives as best we can
Each person has their worth

This class rule is so stupid
In truth it cuts no ice
Your life could change so easily
With just one roll of the dice

So pity not your fellow man
Maybe he pities you
Live out your life for what it's worth
The best way you can do

Why?

There is only one word that resounds in the sky
It is one we all use at some time and it's - 'why?'
Why did it happen? Why did you go?
Why is it raining? Why won't it snow?
Why do the birds fly away once a year?
Why is the pub shut when I want a beer?
Why am I hungry? Why am I sad?
Why do I cry when I'm feeling quite glad?
Why does it hurt so when friends say goodbye?
Why can't things stay as they are - tell me why?

Just three little letters oft said with a sigh
And a glance that looks upwards, *oh why, tell me why?*

Tomorrow

I'm going home tomorrow
I really shouldn't be
Here in this home for aged folk
That term just can't mean me
How can they say I'm fragile?
That alone I cannot cope?
I'm going home tomorrow
At least that's what I hope
Have they the right to put me here?
I really don't feel old
They say I'm hyper-something
That my body's growing cold
But I've got a house, my dog, my cat
Are waiting there for me
I'm going home tomorrow
If I ever find my key
I know I don't remember when
I last had ought to eat
And sometimes when I look down
I see odd shoes on my feet
But I have lived a long life
And there's knowledge I can share
I'm going home tomorrow
If someone will take me there

The House Of Forgotten People

They roam around within the walls
Their days melt into weeks
And nothing quite gets through to them
What can it be they seek?

Maybe they look to find their past
A friend from long ago
A mum, a dad, could be a child
I'd really like to know

Could be a house
Where first they lived
Once filled with love and joy
Where children played at hide-and-seek
And shared their favourite toy

Yet now they wander up and down
So restless and so lonely
Perhaps these words run through their minds
'If only, Lord, if only'

For now their lives are ruled by fate
They're caged in like a mouse
In that place of forgotten people
That resembles so, a house.

The Mirror

I look in the mirror and all I can see
Is the fresh-faced young bride that I know was once me
Laughing and happy, my husband and I
Vowing to love till the day that we die
Along came the children, our lives were complete
We both listened with joy to the sound of small feet

I look in the mirror and now I can see
A middle-aged woman I know once was me
Still smiling, still happy, a sprinkling of grey
The children all grown and now moving away

I look in the mirror and now all I see
A mature grey-haired lady that I know is me
A whimsical smile now resides on my face
Our grandchildren grow at a frightening pace

I look in the mirror and just about see
The very old lady who stares back at me
Our children, their children, grown proud and tall
And I smile at the part that I played in it all

KELLY GIBBONS

I am twenty-three years of age and I live in a town called St Helens.

This will be my second time in Spotlight Poets. I was overwhelmed with being selected to be part of Spotlight Poets 'Express Yourself' in 2005. I have fulfilled my ambition to have my poems published for the public to read and would like to take this opportunity to share more of my work. I have also had poems published in 'Beauty At Our Fingertips' and Poetry Now North and North West England 2004 (for which I have Forward Press to thank).

Since I can remember, writing and reading poetry has been a very pleasurable pastime of mine. Poetry helps me to relax when reading it and helps to work my emotions out when writing it.

I currently have a full-time job as an assistant manager and am studying for an NVQ in Shop Retail Management and for a Professional Jewellers diploma, so finding time for poetry is becoming increasingly more difficult. I often find myself unable to sleep because I have a repetitive sentence in my head that has come from a situation I have been in. I leave pen and paper near my bed so I can capture the words as they materialise, which eases me into sleep. This is how many of my poems are created.

The poems I have selected have been a result of many different influences. For example, nights out in my local town; the loss of a loved one and festive days throughout the year.

Night Out

A twinkle in the eye
From a well-dressed guy
Across a crowded space
Moving in the rat race.
A second look overhead
The look you dread
Swiftly walking near
Music blasting, unable to hear.
A whisper of sweet nothing
A feeling of longing.
An unfamiliar touch
It may get too much.
An obligatory smile
A thought of denial.
A faraway retreat
Smells so sweet.
Bored of empty head
Thinking of my bed
Want to go home
Hands start to roam.
Slap the touch away
Nothing left to say.
Unable to shout
That was my night out.

Creatures Of The Night

I'm like a bee,
Buzzing at the thought of enjoyment.

I'm like a swan,
Preening myself for all to see.

I'm like a sardine,
Squashed in a space full of strangers.

I'm like a tiger,
On the prowl for a lifetime of fun.

I'm like a hyena,
Laughing at every sight and sound.

I'm like a fly,
Seeing duplicate of everything.

I'm like a cat,
Choking on my latest fur ball.

I'm like a slug,
Slowly crawling home.

Kiss

Ohh, come here, my man,
Let me plant one on your mush.
Let me lick those plump red smackers
While I pinch your firm round tush.

Ohh, come here, my man,
Give me a smoochy woochy
And I will slobber wobber
On your la bouche,
My little poochy.

Ohh, come here, my man,
I'm dribbling with excitement.
This moment I can't miss,
When we kiss.

Home Time

The street is dark,
Hardly lit up by the light posts and the passing traffic.
Groups of people everywhere:
Loud, semi-naked and intoxicated.
Eyes glance in your direction.
You look away quickly, hoping not to be noticed and end up involved in a
    fight or attack.
Bright yellow policemen all around,
But we are still unsure whether to feel safe.
They're sat in their vans watching the clock for the end of their shift.
Walking pace quickens.
Goose pimples invade your being.
Tight grip on your belongings,
Feeling dizzy, eyes glazed.
Nearly there now.
Hard to enter the tiny room with two seats and twenty bodies standing round.
'Home please,' I ask the lady.
Beep! Beep!

Resolution

No more chocolate
Not another cig.
No late nights
Drunkenly dancing a jig.

No shouting at the kids
Not another takeaway meal.
No thinking of myself
But understanding how others feel.

No spending all my money
Not another lavish jewel.
No sunbeds twice a week
Try not to look like a fool.

This is my resolution
This year I'll make a stand.
But without all these silly things
Won't my life be bland?

A Woman's Work Is Never Done

I wake up in the morning.
I wash small hands and feet.
I iron uniforms neatly
And walk them down the street.
I clean up breakfast's mess
And hoover tantrum's floor.
I make the tiny beds
And wipe down fingerprints' door.
I place fabric in the machine
Pressing buttons as I go.
Mop tiles with bleach
And holey clothes, I sew.
And when all jobs are done
I've just sat down but then . . .
The wife is home from work
And it starts all over again.

Untitled

When all is said and done
And pain is no more
A newborn is welcomed with a dove's high soar.
And someone who once was
Hovers close with a smile
And follows your path
Be it metre or mile.

Quiet moments feel familiar
As remembrance occurs
Of the joy and happiness
That once was shared.
And the memories live on in the thick of your bone,
As your faith has reassured you:
Be it land or sky, you're not alone.

Forgiveness

I hope that one day,
He'll see me for the girl that I am,
And not like all the others he's had
That only hurt him.
And one day,
When he sees me for the girl that I am
He'll understand that there's only love in my heart
And it's all for him.

And I'll admit that mistakes have been made
But to hurt him was never the game,
I'm just a girl who needs to be loved
And if that means that leaving's the way,
Even though I hope he'll beg me to stay,
He never does, 'cause in his life pride has a big part to play.

One day,
He'll know me more than ever before
And understand why I broke his heart,
To realise that I can mend it too.

I just hope that one day,
When he sees me for the girl that I am,
I'm still around to still want him
Or all the fooling around he that he has done
Would have been for nothing.

Maybe,
All the lies that he's told
Will eventually unfold
And I will realise that I never knew him at all.

Then one day,
I'll see him for the man that he is
And not the loving man I thought he was
And it would have all been for nothing.

But maybe,
When he sees his nasty ways,
He'll forget those horrible days:
Forget himself
And forgive me.

Purse Poem

I am your purse poem
Never to leave your side
No matter how many miles you go
However far or wide.

I'm here to remind you
That no matter where you roam
There's someone thinking of you
Someone you can call home.

And if you ever have a thought for that 'special someone'
You can root me out and read me
I'll make you feel you're not alone

But loved and wanted dearly
And wishing you all the best
And hoping you do the things you want
Don't settle for anything less.

And even though your future may change from day-to-day
This 'special someone's' love and care
Will always stay the same.

Untitled

You've turned my life around
And made me feel alive
And you're the only one
I need by my side.

And when I wake and see you there
I think it's still a dream.
I pinch myself and close my eyes
It's hard for me to breathe.

I've waited so long for this moment
I'll savour while I can.
I'm all aglow,
I want you more -
You've made me what I am.

Dear Lover

I send you this letter
Sealed with a kiss
Of a love so tender
That I will miss.

I send you this letter
Straight from the heart
That being over is for the best
That is why we must part.

I send you this letter
Because even though you care
I won't always be there.

I send you this letter
With thoughts of you
I'm sorry it's over
There's nothing you can do.

I send you this letter
Sealed with a kiss
Of a love so tender
That I'll try and miss.

BERYL DOBSON

Beryl Dobson, born in South Yorkshire, is a housewife, now retired from a life in a wide variety of careers from tax officer to wages clerk to costing and purchasing clerk. She has three children and six grandchildren.

Her hobbies include sewing, reading, gardening and listening to music, both live and recorded. In her younger days she loved sports, and in 1997 she ran the London Marathon for the 'Heart Foundation' raising £1,360 in sponsorship.

Expressions

Expressions, don't they reveal so much?
The innocent look on a child's face
Or that same face
Defiant, bland and stubborn.

Or angry with temper
Wild or horrified too
Wilful, mean or as vacant as can be
Or majestic, regal, pompous and pious
Which shall it be?

Kindly, helpful, pitying and good
Showing all the best things
Do you think I could?

There are numerous expressions
Too many to dwell on for long
The expression of joy, and of living
When you're about to burst into song.

The jealousy of a lover
Is laid bare with a single glance
And the tender eyes
And moving lips
Perhaps will reveal romance.

The stony stare
And the coldness it brings
And the happy smile
And laughter that rings.

The face of sorrow
And unhappiness within
Of compassion and loneliness
With a smile so thin.

The face of pain
Of hate and woe
All these things are known
By the expressions we show.

If I Could Only . . .

If I could only reach to touch you
If I could only feel your hand in mine
If I could only feel your soft lips
Forever embracing mine.

If I could only look into your eyes
What wonders would I see?
If I could only hold you close to me
Then I would be, as rich as could be.

And if only I could whisper . . .
Some sweet words
Into your loving ears

Then maybe, *just* maybe
Because, I'll go on hoping
That there'll be a 'sometime', for me,
Year after year . . .

Why?

Why cannot love be
smooth and tender
like murmurings
in a stream?

Why must it bring
a companion of gloom
that my hasty heart
. . . lets in?

Why in the cloak
of innocence, brought
torment leaves havoc
and makes one distraught?

But if I whisper
. . . a sweet refrain
I hope to find
the calmness again.

All I Ask Of You

All I ask of you
Is true devotion
For my love for you
Is as deep as any ocean.

And all I ask of you
Is sweet contentment
For that is something
That is very hard to find.

And all I ask is . . .
Summer in winter
So that sunshine will abound
Where we live.

And all I ask - is utter bliss
With no dark clouds hovering near
For the love that I have -
I will give you - each and every year.

Strangers

For a moment, my heart stood still,
I guess when I see you
It always will.
Your certain glance,
Your certain smile,
Will always linger
With me awhile.

If only you'd said you loved me,
If only you'd said you cared,
We wouldn't be as strangers
But as one,
With never a care.

And we could have
Journeyed life together,
Sharing happiness and sorrow too,
But those steps
Will never be taken,
Because you have someone new.

Brush Away

Let's brush away
The dark clouds
And replace them
With sunny skies

Let's take away
The sadness
And put laughter
In disguise

From a picture of gloom
To a picture of joy
That's how life's pattern is
For *us* to employ.

For we can change *our* outlook
If only we would try
And then change bad to good
In the twinkling of an eye.

I Remember

I remember spring
But most of all . . .
I remember, everything
. . . about you

I remember
Walking in the rain
I remember
When winter came again
But most of all . . .
. . . I remember you

I remember, those rainbows
         - in the sky
I remember those months
         - that flew by

But most of *all*
That *I* recall
I remember *you!*

When Love Walked In

Like the moonlight's ray
On a dusky night
Softly stealing along its way
Shining bright - till the light of day.
Yes, that's how your love came to stay.

With the shadows of eventide,
And the silence of the sky
Your love winged in . . .
To catch me unawares, yes *I*.

For Venus brought you to me
A love so rare
To cherish and to treasure
I will, for I need you
To be just *there!*

Take Off

Take off thy cloak of darkness
And bid the rising sun
Take off thy mask of innocence
Let thy will be done.

Take off the veil of secrecy
Let all your secrets out
Unseal your lips
Shed away any doubts.

Take off your garb of righteousness
Don one of gaiety
Take off your role of sinner
Take one of piety.

And take off thy shroud
Of gloom and doubt
Put on one to reason
Everything out - *take off!*

Seasons Of My Years

In the *spring* of my years
Full of youth and zest
Living life so joyfully
Fulfilling every quest.

Meeting every challenge
Reaching for every goal
Taking life's gifts, to enjoy
And employ, from my very soul.

And in the *summer* of my years
A little wiser it appears
Still being ever moulded
To my innermost desires.

And the hand that steers the helm -
Through the voyage of time
Learning every lesson
Through folly and love sublime.

And now in the *September* of my years
I've gathered my harvest
With laughter and tears.

Met every inward struggle
Journeyed on an upward path
With sweet contentment
Dispersing clouds of wrath.

And in the *winter* of my years
I'm buffeted by every storm
My faltering steps - lead me on
To the future, now misty and dim.

So calm, so peaceful
A haven I seek
All dangers seem past
And I'm so meek.

And in the *river* of my years
I glide swiftly onwards
To that safe retreat.

Heartbeats

Listen to the beating
- of my heart
No tide of joy was trod
- so carefully.

For they are murmurings
- soft and low
Within, of you
Forever be.

For love came to me
And found me lonely
And the conquest was never seen
To you - but to *me*, only.

And with each measured beat
I have a mystic sigh
And cheerily plod on
To that rainbow in the sky.

No chartered course
Was ever set
No prize so rare
- was sought.

For the love, that was -
Bestowed - on me
I'm sure
Was Heaven-wrought.

We Will

We will go to Never Land
Where we have been before
We will go to Never Land
Where we know the score.

We will never go to Never Land
Where we *never* ever meet
And where I *never* see you
On *any* kind of street.

For when I go to Never Land
I know the answer's *'No!'*
So I might as well save - a journey
For something, I *already* know.

ELLEN SPIRING

I am a retired health visitor of 57 years of age. My occupation as a nurse commenced when I was the tender age of sixteen and I have worked in the NHS since then, in curative medicine.

On the death of my father, due to cancer, I changed my thinking to prevention and took a change of direction in my career. I subsequently gained more qualifications to obtain, at degree level, the 'Health Visitor's' certificate.

As a family person, I get a lot of my inspiration from them. They are my subjects, in particular my son and daughter and two grandsons. I also love the countryside and I am fortunate enough to live in a rural area, near my beloved Pendle Hill and Ribble Valley. Pendle and its folklore figure a lot in my poetry and stories. I currently attend a creative writing course and have done so for about two years. This has given me a new dimension alongside that of arts and crafts. Art is an ongoing interest too, mostly watercolour painting. I like to think that it has improved my writing, as the written word is comparable to a blank canvas and the words can paint a picture just as compelling and dramatic. They complement one another well.

I was born in Dublin, Eire. My mother is Irish, consequently I have an Irish family. Lots of my stories are about them but the names have been changed to protect the innocent.

At certain times in my life I have experienced many challenges and my writing has proved a therapeutic tool and a valuable coping mechanism. I am a Christian and I try to express my spiritual belief in my poetry and rhyme. I enjoy keeping fit, it has always been a part of my routine to do gym and swim. I walk the hills in the Pendle area. This helps to paint a picture in words.

The friends I have made at the leisure centre are quite often the butt of my quirky sense of humour in my poems. Being fans of Blackburn Rovers foot team, they get a mention in the local rag.

My life is quite full because of my family, my writing and my hobbies. I think my work reflects this. I hope I am successful in this, if not I will carry on doing what I like doing, in the hope that my work will be appreciated for its humour and candour.

My Irish Rose

Long nut-brown hair she had.
A lovely sight to see.
The biggest, bluest eyes she had.
She thought to capture me.

Capture me she did, I fell in love.
A fervent prayer I sent to up above.
'Please, dear Lord, let her stay
Let my new love not go away.'

That was all of thirty years ago,
The sight of her still makes my heart glow.
There are two children now, one girl, one boy.
I was never a man to be so coy.

We married for love and kindled a flame.
Her looks, her eyes, her hair to blame.
Our little girl, very like her mother.
Likewise the boy, her little brother.

Across the table she looks at me.
My life, my love, it was meant to be.
Her long nut-brown hair now streaked with grey.
Her big blue eyes won't go away.

My Irish rose without a thorn.
Never a wrong word, never any scorn.
'Please, Lord, let her longer stay
Let the love of my life not go away.'

The Odd Couple

We both work hard; in different ways toil.
Another couple we would not spoil.
For him, his first love is his cricket.
He is not happy out of sight of a wicket.
The cricket season's over and I think he's mine.
No, he's in a deep decline.

When I hope he'll be a 'born-again rocker',
He takes consolation in a game called soccer.
Rugby is another choice,
My protests I could loudly voice.
'What is the point?' I ask you, friend.
The TV and radio win in the end.

Is there any action I should take?
Go into a domestic state.
Get into the kitchen, bake a pie or a cake.
Iron his shirts, sew his clothes.
Perhaps take on another pose.

Take myself to the garden with a hoe and a rake.
No, that backache I cannot fake.
'Grin and bear it' so I'm told.
But I'm middle-aged and not 'that' old.
In fact I can be quite a 'mover'.
In modern terms called a 'bit of a groover'.

So with 'the ageing process' and passing of time,
I hope another like me appreciates rhyme.
I wish another as candid as me,
Will take up a pen and be word free.
I hope that they can well afford,
To prove that 'the pen is mightier than the sword'.

Lucy

Lucy was my daughter's dog, a spaniel by breed.
She was a fussy canine when you had her to feed.
Nothing but the best, that Lucy dog would eat.
Black and white with spotted legs, her tail and her feet.
With bright brown eyes she used to plead
To beg her biscuits and haute cuisine feed.

She was an obedient dog and would do tricks.
Took a lot of notice, and then gave you licks.
She'd wash your face with her pink tongue.
Wanted her 'walkies' but played out too long.
We were tired out by the time she'd done.
Running for a stick, the newspaper she'd bring home,

It was a little worse for wear for all her chewing.
With the other male dogs, Lucy took to wooing.
A bonny lass this pedigree dog.
At night in her basket she slept like a log.
No howling disturbing, as quiet as a mouse.
Yet what a performance if a stranger came near the house.

As soft as butter, she loved the fuss.
But most all she loved all of us.

Dad's Anniversary

A dad is a dad when all is said and done.
I know, like you, I had a wonderful one.
He was taken away, no longer there.
A disease called cancer, that wasn't fair.

This is the time when you miss your dad the most,
His anniversary dawns and you're feeling lost.
The memories come, hopefully most are good.
A special memorial to him if you could.

A flower, a poem left in a special place
Will bring you, Alan, a smile to your face.
To think of him fondly in your mind's eye.
Because, my dear, you can never say goodbye.
A dad is a dad when all is said and done.
I know, like you, I had a wonderful one.

Much love at this time,

Ellen

The Written Word

Write down something every day.
Let not your thoughts go away.
Find yourself some paper and a pen.
Write a story, a story beginning 'Remember when?'
It may be of love, it may be of strife.
Of a husband, a partner, a lover or wife.

What an art this is writing to remember.
A month, a year, a day in September.
When times were good and had to be had.
Days that were worse, that left you feeling bad.
Looking towards tomorrow with no solution.
Trials, tribulations and fear of retribution.

Yet what of the times, the times that matter?
You found answers in coping, yourself could flatter.
You looked towards compassion, 'make do and mend',
Perhaps all you needed was one true friend.
To 'talk out' the problems and point the way.
Rub ointment on wounds, say 'Have a good day'.

Molly

My special friend owns a cat named Molly.
She burns her tail for her folly.
As too near the gas fire she goes.
Moll's even burned her little toes.

When lazing by the fire her black tail she unfurls.
In-between the protective mesh, her tail into the flames she curls.
The burnt fur singeing alerts her master.
It is all done in seconds, he cannot move faster.

The firebricks are all now black, dear me, alas, alack.
The 'Scrubright' cleaner he has to use applied with a toothbrush.
Molly is in disgrace, under the sideboard she does rush.
Now there's a silence and a hush.

Will she try his patience once again?
Will she once more risk the pain?
Burn and singe her big black tail.
Her master's efforts to stop her fail.

Curled around then into the flame.
Her sorry owner takes the blame.

I came up with a bright idea to foil this silly cat.
A 'sort of makeshift' fireguard was put up and that was that.
We will have to wait to see any success.
Her master is heartily sick of cleaning the black mess.

To say nothing about the smell of 'singe'
It's enough to make a grown man cringe.

Valentine Verse

Roses are red, violets are blue.
It all begins and ends with you.
Will you say yes and be mine,
My very eldest valentine?

'We' are only just but one year old.
Perhaps I shouldn't be so bold,
But life is too short not to say,
What I feel for you today.

'50+' is our age group, others call us 'Wrinklies',
They're really only 'laughter lines' often called 'crinklies'.
What do they know of 'middle-aged' love?
At least it shines from high above.

Steadfast and true, I will love you,
In fact I'll make you feel brand new.
When you take me in your arms,
At least I feel your wonderful charms.

Roses are red, violets are blue.
It all begins and ends with you.
Will you say yes and be mine,
My over-50's valentine?

The Secret Garden

There are three large oak trees behind the garden wall.
Two ash trees have grown, not so tall.
A solitary apple tree bearing rosy red fruit.
This was once a sapling I trod with my boot.

At the far garden wall a trellis tells a story.
Rambling clematis and sweet jasmine in all their glory.
Entwining the fence a maroon passion flower.
A statue and a fountain complete with water power.

Between the walls the lush grass grows.
Feeling soft, looking green between my toes.
Geraniums in pots, coloured orange and pink.
Yellow hollyhocks and delphiniums, the colour of ink.

Their different perfumes pervade the air.
As for myself I stand and stare.
I think of the past times I shared with another.
My sweetheart long dead, I yearn for my lover.

He planted two roses for me years ago.
The blooms, red and peach, in abundance do grow.
The memories flow back, I start to cry.
The war took him from me. Why did he die?

A small stone seat stands under an arch.
Honeysuckle adorns it and climbs up the larch.
The bees are humming, the butterflies flitter.
From branch to branch, the birds fly and twitter.

Into a small pond the fountain trickles.
I step into the water, my toes it tickles.
He and I used to paddle in days gone by.
The memories flood back, I start to cry.

There is a black and white cat stretched out in the sun.
No war in this garden, that war was won.
I see all the colours, all the perfumes I love.
I think of my sweetheart now up above.

I hope that he sees me through his spirit eyes.
I hope, too, that he is restful beyond the skies.
Our secret garden is precious, sweet memories we did share.
When my love and I, one another would share.

Modern Day War?

Mega war, mega war, out, out, out.
Hear new era, era, shout, shout, shout.
Class-orientated, is it or not?
Are we going there again?
Has the world learned nothing. Refrain.
Yes, refrain is when we'll learn.
From pushing politics we do yearn.
It has historically happened before.
Are we going to take the world to the floor?
Too young they are to know past war.
Until they know, what is it all for?
The older generation can tell the tale.
They suffered, loved and lost.
In their eyes we pale.
Pale in significance of what they knew.
When actions bore the loss of more than a few.
You youngsters know nothing of the real thing.
Past veterans and parents suffered everything.
They see it happen all again.
More violence in a different way.
Why the hell put up and stay?

ARTHUR

Born into a mining family in sunny South Wales and coming from generations of mining and farming folk, I feel my history has left its mark on me. I have a reputation for being militant. So much so, after I had been filmed by the BBC, they dubbed me as the most militant man in Wales while my nicknames were Gary the Red in the mine I worked and Arthur Scargill as my years I served as a postman. I also feel that having been born prematurely has left me with traits that augment, complementing my militancy with an exigency I have little control over. These tendencies, I believe, are the fuel for my creativity by giving me my inspiration, while I use my family, especially my wife, Pam, as a template with which I then draw from my experience of nature in general.

I began composing poetry while convalescing after suffering a nervous breakdown and many of my poems are based on what I have seen at mental units and some of the many people I have met who suffer mental illness. I find it alleviates my own suffering too. I suffer from manic depression but, in addition, possess a fully developing photographic memory at the same time.

My recurring themes are, without doubt, love and nature and I derive immense pleasure in composing a romantic poem that is of some worth or merit. On this occasion, my second bite at Spotlight Poets, after experiencing four family bereavements, I have composed my collection on a theme of the cycle of life, a kind of love, promise, environment, weddings and funerals, commemorating our moments of grief at the same time.

If I am attempting to raise consciousness it is to make people aware of their mortality as my family and I have suddenly become aware of ours.

A Heavy Load

(Composed in loving memory of Gareth Hurley 28/2/77-26/2/06)

When we tragically lose a loved one,
We feel the most excruciating pain,
While life is suddenly bereft of any fun
For all the grief, our hearts and souls must sustain.

One does not know whether to turn or run,
It's so inexplicable one simply can't explain,
Thoughts frozen while words remain unspoken
'Twixt compulsion and reluctance to complain.

But if this old life is to offer any token
Then the abiding grief of a heart shall wane,
Then our broken hearts shall once more see the sun,
Allowing laughter into our souls once again.

Yet when the loss is beyond all consoling then
The heart asks why the meek and innocent are slain.
But as days go by the heavy load will softly lighten
As with anguish our heavy hearts learn how to contain.

The memories of a loved one will then quite often,
With the passage of time, cheerfully entertain,
That is not to say the grief will ever be forgotten
But will strengthen us while bearing under the strain.

For Gareth you were so full of fun, quite insane!
In fact you couldn't have been any madder!
So often you would have us laughing like a drain,
That is why this tale couldn't be any sadder.

What makes it such an injustice, quite simple and plain!
Is that you departed from this Earth as young as you were
And adding to the grief of the stunned heart's pain
You leave behind your pride in your young son and lover.

Our pitiful grief-stricken hearts call out in vain
While finding it hard to believe you are no more,
But we will remember you as a rainbow in the rain
Once all the Heaven and earthly tears cease to pour.

Arthur

Do They Bloom In Heaven Too?

Unable to explain away my grief and gloom,
I take great comfort when I see daffodils in bloom,
For with the arrival of grand nature's spring,
I remember you and all the joy you used to bring.

Even though while nodding their noble trumpets so gay,
It was the time that you were so cruelly taken away,
Just like a noble daffodil, you lit up everyone's life,
That is the reason why I consented to become your wife.

Each and every year they shall be a remembrance,
As a living token of our brief, loving romance!
Gareth, do they bloom up in Heaven too?
You can tell me one day when I meet up with you.

But until that fateful day finally arrives
Your living memory shall light up our lives,
And when the anniversary of your passing looms,
I shall think of you as hosts of daffodil blooms.

And when spring rainbows light up the heavens above
I shall imagine it's you blessing us with your love,
Watching over us both with gentle, loving care,
So in that way I know you will always be there.

Although our infant son is yet far too young
To understand, for his life has only just begun,
I shall explain if only to ease the loss and pain,
In noble daffodils and spring rainbows in the rain.

And when he is old enough to comprehend,
I shall describe how, from above, the love you send,
Is part of nature embracing us both so dearly,
Just as you always did so endearingly!

You gave me so many things to remember you by
And in my grief I have to ask myself why?
Noble as a daffodil, colourful as a rainbow,
You were a wonderful man to love and know.

Arthur

Mercy

How I remember my father's final, fateful hour
As he struggled, gasping for breath so bitter and sour.
When the canon approached him with God's power
His whole body shrank away as he began to cower.

Mere words of comfort the canon was about to lend
So to Heaven, his dark, lost soul he could send,
But my father chose to die without such a friend
Staying an atheist right to the very end.

Never in life did he ever lack in spirit
But simply did not appreciate the good canon's visit.
A lifelong miner, religion he would not admit
For in his scheme of things, God just did not fit.

Yet I still think of him up there in Heaven
Although I couldn't quite see it like that then,
When with his eyes the good canon he did so condemn
But for sure, God has mercy for such lonely men.

Whenever I pray or sing a carol at Christmas
My fragile heart feels it is entirely made of glass,
So I think of him in nature, in every blade of grass
While believing that into Heaven his lonely soul did pass.

Arthur

How Much Do You Love Me?

You question how much my red heart loves you
Putting to test a bond of love that is true.
Before you consented it was cold, lonely and blue,
Now it passionately beats romantic blood anew.

How it mingles with the stars of the night sky
While everything it sees is such a wondrous sight,
For somehow your love has taught it how to fly
Underneath the glimmer of this silver moonlight!

Looking at you, how I believe in angels,
Wishes coming true and even in magic:
For all the gloom in the world your love dispels
And to lose such a thing would be truly tragic.

No trophy could ever compare with your beauty,
You are a lady of elegance and grace
And I feel I would be neglecting my duty
If I wasn't honest and told you face to face.

You are all the riches a man could wish to acquire
And I cherish you, appreciating your true worth,
That's why, darling, you're my grateful heart's desire,
You've just made a heaven for me right here on Earth.

It's a kingdom where my spirit may roam freely
For your love makes me as happy as a king.
I solemnly promise to always love you dearly
As on bended knee I present this engagement ring.

We'll stay together forever, whatever the grief or strife,
Therefore our love shall blossom into a love divine.
I pledge to you a humble red heart, my soul, my life,
Upon this heaven-sent day of old St Valentine!

Arthur

Hailing Heaven

My gushing, red heart is so full of glee
It hails Heaven with romantic song!
For she has just said that she loves me.
Words it has waited to hear for so long.

And now as through Heaven I tread
Along valleys, amongst angels, choirs and kings,
I pay tribute to all! Alive and dead;
Expressing thanks for my God-given wings.

When my conscience returns to old Mother Earth,
I will honour with pride the land of my family.
I promise to work hard to prove my worth,
Now true love has set my yearning heart free.

Thank you, to all you fallen souls of conflict
For procuring my legacy of freedom!
For enduring the pain and suffering Hell will inflict
In creating such a Heavenly Kingdom.

With this lesson of love I've received I can
Preach to the long, the short and the tall.
To be a big man you must stay a little man:
Or one shall grow out of reach of the small.

Arthur

Why?

Whosoever saves a single life
Is as if he had saved the whole world.
Whosoever destroys a single life
Is as if he had destroyed the whole world.

How these words echo in my ears,
So profound, they have poignancy.
They help while fighting back the tears,
Good philosophy I fancy.

Time's fateful hour has at last come.
That dreadful moment has approached.
My sweating body has gone numb
As the macabre subject is broached.

This, the final act of our love.
We are not witnessing murder
But caring hands that gently shove
To save agonies that pain her.

Frugally we've saved up morphine,
Enough to send her to Heaven.
To the world it may seem obscene
But our love's about to ripen.

Fifty short years we've known each other
And we still think we're in our prime.
But for this merciless cancer
I wouldn't commit this heinous crime.

As she loses all consciousness
I know that she is gone forever.
So long she had fought her sickness
And now I intend to join her.

Though she won't be expecting me
I'll surprise her and when she asks why
I'll just explain to her simply,
I couldn't bear to say goodbye.

Arthur

Humanity

Spirit Series. Lessons in Love

Humanity could not survive for a single day
But for love, a very wise man once said,
But there doesn't seem much of it about today
As if passion has lost its lustre and is no longer red!

Lovers no longer court each other in dance
As they once so often did yesteryear,
So one may think life is bereft of romance
And people's love is not held half so dear.

People in general don't seem to be half so kind
Or giving and are fast becoming a selfish creed,
But love is everywhere about us one shall find
Despite all the avarice and greed we breed.

Yet while many dedicate their lives to others
Giving aid and supporting a plethora of charities,
Against such adversity we show our true colours
Levelling out all of our disparities.

Even though it is rare we all concert as one
It is never far beyond our capability,
After all, when all has been said and done
We each and every one make up humanity.

For sure falling in love will last for evermore
But the way we express it should be an art,
As in romantic ages that have gone before
With elegant ladies and gentlemen so smart.

For our hearts and souls were made for loving
We can't help it for it is part of our nature.
If we're not busy giving we are receiving,
A part of a culture we all lovingly nurture.

Humanity could not survive for a single day
But for love, a very wise man once said,
So let us hope that's just the way it'll stay,
Without faith, hope and charity, many tears would be shed.

Arthur

My Love

Do you remember how we romantically planted this rose
And said how we'd both watch as our deepening love grows?
Do you remember how passionately we'd kiss when we watered
Or fed her together while she was being lovingly nurtured?

Do you remember how gaily we both chose her elegant name
Saying how much we loved each other, setting our hearts aflame?
Do you remember our delight when we cut that first scarlet bloom
Giving us a heavenly fragrance that would dispel anybody's gloom?

Do you remember when she began producing her blossom freely?
It coincided with when we were blessed with our little family.
Do you remember last night as the full moon lit the starry sky?
We still tenderly kissed beside her after all these years have gone by.

Arthur

Mona Lisa

Oh Mona Lisa, how you so enthral
With just the merest enigmatic smile.
You look as if you have not loved at all,
Or at least it's been for such a long while.

Do you smile so to entice a romance
So true love you shall eventually find?
Surely a blossoming love has every chance
For one so beautiful who's one of a kind!

Perhaps that's why you smile in your portrait:
Enchanting men all over the whole wide world,
Or is it simply your natural trait
And with it your true beauty is unfurled?

Arthur

None Shall Weep

Another dusk, another dawn and another day!
I'm so tired of living and so scared of passing away.
Life is fast losing its lustre, no longer endearing
As my limbs grow feeble while everything is so wearing.

Outliving families and friends and without children
The daunting prospect of ageing begins to frighten.
Who shall mourn my passing when I mortally meet death?
And just who shall weep when I gasp my last breath?

O I had many chances and often could have wed
But I harboured a cold, selfish heart instead.
Now I feel deep regret but I made my own bed
But who shall spare me a thought after I am dead?

Love was always a stranger in its own way
And for some reason I held it far at bay,
Now I haven't the strength to love anyway
So none shall weep when I do finally pass away.

Arthur

Weep Not For Me
(Spirit Series. A Lament)

Weep not for me in the hour of my passing
For I have experienced a colourful life.
In a vision I see a congregation massing
Who're grieving with mercy for my tearful wife!

My spirit roams about the chapel freely
Praying to God, Heaven my lost soul will take,
As I embrace my family so endearingly
Just like in a dream from which I'm about to awake!

I take heart from the passionate singing
And the respectful way everybody stands.
Great comfort and unity this seems to bring
While the good preacher conducts with both hands.

It was without my consent that I was born
And it was against my will that I died,
In death from this earthly realm my spirit is torn
As I cross over that great heavenly divide.

Now as to the four winds my ashes are scattered
Please remember my humble sense of propriety,
I learned that society really mattered
So to inspire and nurture humanity!

And perhaps some may recall readings of my prose
As sweet whispers upon the Welsh breeze,
So whenever she picks up, rises or blows
Poetry shall be singing throughout the trees.

All the romantic words of love that I composed
I pray on winds be softly spoken for evermore,
For even though my mortal mouth is forever closed
Love filled my heart with such pride, with passion I could roar.

So weep not for me in the hour of my passing
For I have had such a wonderful life,
I have been no angel but committed little sin,
Weep for my grieving family and lost, loving wife.

Arthur

A Tender Kiss

While ambling through the Welsh countryside
Amongst pink and mauve heather in the mist,
The whole wide world seemed to coincide
As the white sky and the earth tenderly kissed.

Then as I climbed to reach the mountain top
I found myself standing above a vast cloud.
It took my breath away, compelling me to stop
To enjoy the spectacle far from the madding crowd!

A magical moment of sheer inspiration
Just like it had been painted by an artist's hand,
Then with a strong sense of self-righteous indignation
I declared Wales a most beautiful land.

And then, when the misty air began to clear
Her long, green valleys opened up before me.
To my warm patriotic heart she felt so dear
That I feel blessed to live in a land so lovely.

Arthur

Information

We hope you have enjoyed reading this book - and that
you will continue to enjoy it in the coming years.

If you are interested in becoming a Spotlight Poet then
drop us a line, or give us a call, and we'll send you a free
information pack.

Alternatively, if you would like to order further copies of
this book or any of our other titles, then please give us a
call or log onto our website at www.forwardpress.co.uk.

Spotlight Poets Information
Remus House
Coltsfoot Drive
Peterborough
PE2 9JX
(01733) 898101